Heart to Heart

Talks with God

A Collection of Inspirational Poetry

Kathryn Kendrick

Kathryn Kenduk
07/25/19

James 4:8a

Heart to Heart
Talks with God
by Kathryn Kendrick

Printed in the United States of America

ISBN 9781498405720

Image Credits

An Empty Vessel – http://flickr.com/photos/kaye13/6261362277/

Whosoever Will - http://www.flickr.com/photos/waitingfortheword/5560612051/

The Depth of God's Love / http://www.atoast2wealth.com/wp- content/uploads/2012/01/Jesus-Christ100.jpgh/lh3.gpht.com/KI31IJrBzQIwvtvYKvUYTtc2V7tVxsvFg=s97two

All Eyes Are Watching You   http://www.4shared.com/photo/D9C3zKM1/beautiful-eyes-ilustrasi-by-is.html

Be Not Deceived http://reflectionandchoice.files.wordpress.com/2014/04/d.jpg?w=352&h=263

Whenever I Call - http://gemsdaily.blogspot.com/2012/04/holding-hands.html

I'll Weep No More - https://lh6.ggpht.com/Suymodtlx03GvGke0_nJWshni3IGIiZKILjKfetT3iL_LYM89V8JyW6ihTCI5f4buR0DP5w=s114

Eternity – http://dlsa9re.wikispaces.com/Heaven's+Guidance

Choose This Day - http://dandylionpages.wordpress.com/2010/11/19/himmelhelvete/

www.xulonpress.com

Jami

May God bless you
and those you love

Kathy

Table of Contents

Preface

Although I always considered myself a Christian, my Christianity did not really extend beyond believing in God and His Son. I had no personal relationship with Jesus other than the "please grant my request" mentality in which so many of us engage. This is often referred to as having head-knowledge, but not heart-knowledge of Jesus Christ or a Christian in name only. Thankfully, even during this long, self-absorbed period of my life, God protected me–mainly from myself. When I decided to establish and pursue a close, personal relationship with God, He was right there waiting to fellowship with me. From that moment on, I was forever changed.

Many times in a Christian's life, there are times of testing. These tests come packaged in many different circumstances and can require varying degrees of struggle and commitment to master. Sometimes tests come to challenge us to stand up and defend what we confess to believe. My most important test to-date came in November 2013, and provided an amazing testimony: The writing of this collection of poetry.

We began to attend a small church where on the surface all seemed 'right with the world.' The people were nice, God touched me in a mighty way, and I was content. I thought I had found my forever church home.

Sadly, things within the church were more 'right with the world' than right with God and his teachings. After a few weeks, a little red flag of warning began to flutter. As more time passed and different people came and went, that little red flag began to wave furiously; so much so, that it became apparent that what was occurring was not Biblical. I felt God wanted me to address the situation. Me, the shy, introvert who had never stood up to anyone over any issue in my entire 58 years, was to confront a seasoned pastor who was allowing sin to remain unchecked in his 'church.' I felt confused, humbled, and very ill-equipped; but at the same time, I **knew** God was calling me to do this.

As humbly, thoughtfully and delicately as I possibly could, I broached the subject with the pastor stating my concerns. He admitted he was fully aware of the situation and my concerns were valid and indeed true. While I was initially placated with his response, something in my spirit remained restless and uncomfortable. Weeks passed, and again, I reached out to discuss this issue with the pastor in an effort to understand the situation from a Biblical perspective.

This second inquiry produced righteous indignation and hostility, wherein the pastor accused me of questioning his knowledge, integrity and leadership. However, he still did not Biblically support his stance on allowing the sin. My contention was/is, if we permit a professing Christian to continue willfully in their pre-conversion sin, while welcoming them into the 'fold,' we are doing them, as well as the rest of the 'church' a disservice. In effectively condoning their sin, we remove the impetus for their repentance and change.

In 1 John 3:9 (NIV) John writes: "No one who is born of God will continue to sin, because God's seed remains in them; they cannot go on sinning, because they have been born of God."

In 1 Corinthians 5:11 (NIV) Paul, an apostle of Christ writes to the church of Corinth: "But now I am writing to you that you must not associate with anyone who claims to be a brother or sister but is sexually immoral or greedy, an idolater or slanderer, a drunkard or swindler. Do not even eat with such people."

Again, in 1 Corinthians 6:9-10 (NIV) Paul writes: "Or do you not know that wrongdoers will not inherit the kingdom of God? Do not be deceived: Neither the sexually immoral nor idolaters nor adulterers nor men who have sex with men nor thieves nor the greedy nor drunkards nor slanderers nor swindlers will inherit the kingdom of God."

Finally, in Romans 6:6-7 (NIV) Paul writes: " For we know that our old self was crucified with him so that the body ruled by sin might be done away with, that we should no longer be slaves to sin, because anyone who has died has been set free from sin."

I could go on, but you get the idea.

Although the outcome was not at all what I anticipated for *I* was the one labeled "toxic" and, subsequently ostracized, I would not change the situation. As a direct result of my obedience and willingness to step out in faith to do what the Father asked of me, He blessed me with this book of poetry.

The poems began gradually with an idea or line that would awaken me in the night. The first time or two I didn't think much of it and simply rolled over and went back to sleep, thinking I would write it down in the morning. The next morning, however, I could not remember the verse I had "memorized" the night before. Realizing that this was something new and special, I quickly learned to get up, get pen and paper and record the words God was imparting or they would be lost forever.

Thus, what began as a thought on the edge of sleep, quickly developed into a stanza, then a complete poem. One after another, the poems kept coming. Often, the words flowed and the poem was quickly finished. At other times, a poem unfolded over hours or even days. Occasionally, the poems came one after another; and once, four separate poems developed simultaneously.

In a short, seven-month period, God's messages grew into an entire book of inspirational, thought-provoking, soul-searching poetry to share with believers and non-believers alike. I take no credit for the content, other than putting pen to paper and pursuing the road to publication, because I know it is God who is imparting the words to me to share with 'whosoever will' partake.

Even as I prepare this book for publication, God continues to fill my head and heart with His words to share. Six or eight new poems were added while completing the editing process. God willing, there will be a follow-up volume.

I would love to know your thoughts on the poems. You may contact me on the *Heart to Heart ~ Talks With God* Facebook page or via email at hearttohearttalkswithgod@gmail.com.

I pray that all who read *Heart To Heart ~ Talks With God* will be touched, changed and richly blessed!

Blessings ~

Kathy

Dedication

This book is dedicated to the memory of my mother and father, Nellie and John Sorensen, Jr., with love and appreciation for raising their children in the fear and admonition of God, providing a spiritual foundation for us to build upon ourselves.

I can't wait to see you both at The Gate!

Daddy created this inspiring double exposure picture while attending photography school in Dallas, Texas in 1947. It lovingly hangs in a place of prominence in my home.

Acknowledgments

I thank God for using me as His vessel to convey His messages through this book of poetry.

Thanks to my cousin, Barbara Hite, for giving me a copy of the New International Study Bible. Your gift resulted in a new phase of my spiritual journey, which laid the foundation for this book. The Bible tells us in James 4:8 (NIV) "Come near to God and he will come near to you." Over the past year, the truth of these words has resonated strongly in my life.

A heartfelt thank you to all those who have encouraged and supported me in this endeavor–Betty W. Bishop, Barbara Corrie, Weslie Kendrick Fox, Lisa Hafer Hite, Junie Jenkinson, Wendy West Minotti, Gail Rohr Sorensen, and Sharon Hamrick Tyler. Your reassurance kept me moving forward when my spirit began to question or doubt.

In addition, a very special thank you to my soul mate and husband of 34 years, Wes Kendrick, as well as my friend, Florence O'Connor for their proofreading services and to my "sister" Pauleitta Kendrick Phillips for her editorial services.

An Empty Vessel

But we have this treasure in jars of clay to show that this all-surpassing power is from God and not from us. 2 Corinthians 4:7

My sheep listen to my voice; I know them, and they follow me. John 10:27

But store up for yourselves treasures in heaven, where moths and vermin do not destroy, and where thieves do not break in and steal. For where your treasure is, there your heart will be also. Matthew 6:20-21

His master replied, 'Well done, good and faithful servant! You have been faithful with a few things; I will put you in charge of many things. Come and share in your master's happiness!' Matthew 25:21

Well Done, Faithful One

Line by line
and day by day,
I wrote each word, Lord
that You conveyed.

I shared them all
in this little book,
I pray those who need them
will stop and take a look.

You've done Your part
and I've done mine,
The rest of the story
will unfold over time.

I pray those who read it
are forever changed,
Their souls redirected
and lives rearranged.

I pray the lost
receive salvation,
And saints receive
new revelation.

May those who read it
be richly blessed,
May the words within
help them through life's tests.

And when my time
on earth is done,
I'll hear You say
"Well done, faithful one!"

April 24, 2014

Deep in the Night

In the still of night
before asleep I fall,
It's in this quiet time
that I hear God's voice call.

Or from a deep slumber
I gradually awake,
Faced with a decision
only I can make.

So I rouse from sleep
and rise from my bed,
Listening intently
to His voice in my head.

With paper and pen
I begin to write,
As God inspires me
deep in the night.

He fills my mind
and heart with His thoughts,
I must write quickly
or the words will be lost.

Some words flow quickly
and cannot be restrained,
Others trickle gently
like a soft, summer rain.

I've learned to recognize
and listen to His voice,
For hearing from God
makes my spirit rejoice.

March 17, 2014

An Empty Vessel

When I think there are
no words left to say,
God gives me an idea
that just won't go away.

I frantically scribble
so no words will be lost,
I must do His will
whatever the cost.

I give God all the glory
for I know it is He,
I've tried on my own
but no words come to me.

I am the vessel
He's chosen to use,
I write His poetry
and share the Good News.

God's always looking
for a willing heart,
Who'll do His will
by playing their part.

An empty vessel
He'll fill to the brim,
When we humble ourselves
and surrender to Him.

One act of obedience
reaped amazing benefit,
I will not give up
I cannot quit.

So use me Lord
as You will,
You've given me much
yet I hunger still;

To do Your work
and know Your will,
An empty vessel
only You can fill.

March 26, 2014

Whosoever Will

Here I am! Behold, I stand at the door, and knock. If anyone hears my voice, and opens the door, I will come and eat with that person, and they with me. Revelation 3:20

The eyes of the arrogant will be humbled and human pride brought low; the LORD alone will be exalted in that day. The LORD Almighty has a day in store for all the proud and lofty, for all that is exalted (and they will be humbled), Isaiah 2:11-12

He [Jesus] said to them, "Go into all the world and preach the gospel to all creation. Whoever believes and is baptized will be saved, but whoever does not believe will be condemned. Mark 16:15-16

Jesus said to them, "A prophet is not without honor except in his own town, among his relatives and in his own home." Mark 6:4

Whosoever Will

There are times we all question
what we can't see or touch,
To believe in the unseen
can prove to be too much.

But faith comes by hearing
the words of God's truth,
And recalling the stories
we've heard from our youth.

When we humbly seek
to know God's heart,
His wisdom and love
He'll graciously impart.

God wants us to know Him
and seek His face,
He wants to pour out His blessings
of abundance and grace.

But God will not intrude
where He's not invited,
In rejecting His love
we're the one who is slighted.

We forfeit an inheritance
of eternal life,
Traded for worldly pleasures
and a life filled with strife.

It is God's will
that none should be lost,
Salvation is a gift
for which Jesus paid the cost.

Whosoever will
is welcome to come,
To God, the Father
through Jesus, His Son.

Won't you open your heart
and welcome Him in?
For Jesus alone
can forgive all your sin!

He's watching and waiting
this very hour,
To fill you with His love
His wisdom and power.

May 19, 2014

Take a Stand

Lest we live awhile in darkness -
Can we appreciate the light?
Lest we experience being wronged -
Can we realize what is right?

Lest we journey through the valley -
Can we soar on wings of eagles?
Lest we wear a crown of thorns -
Can we earn a crown more regal?

When sorrows come
and you don't understand,
Just reach out to Jesus
He'll take your hand.

For pain and suffering
are nothing new,
They come to each of us
when our time is due.

You must be prepared
to run the race,
And when hard times come
you must seek His face.

For in Him you will find
comfort and peace,
Wrapped securely in His arms
you'll find sweet release.

You can let down your guard
and pour out your heart,
His love endures forever
and will not depart.

A friend to sinners
and saints alike,
For you and me
Jesus laid down His life.

We were never meant to go
through this life alone,
Our future with Him secured
when they rolled away the stone.

Jesus is waiting -
He's given an invitation,
To every man, woman and child
of every tribe and nation.

The decision is personal
one we each must make,
Won't you choose Jesus now
before it's too late?

You'll never regret it
and never look back,
When you're living for Jesus
you're on the right track.

Your future will be assured
your heavenly home prepared,
He'll meet you at Heaven's Gate
or meet you in the air.

The choice is up to you my friend,
but you must take a stand,
Will you spend eternity in darkness,
or seated at Jesus' right hand?

February 16, 2014

Surrender Your Heart

God uses His children
to convey His heart,
In writing His words
I'm doing my part.

In the words I write
God is speaking to you,
To write them and share
is what I must do.

I pray His words
resonate in your heart,
Compelling you now
to make a new start.

It is God's will
that all should believe,
In rejecting His Son
you cause God to grieve.

We all have sinned
and fall short of His glory,
By surrendering to Jesus
you can rewrite your story.

For Jesus alone
can redeem us from sin,
And give us new life
to live eternally with Him.

He wants to break down
your walls of pride,
And heal all the pain
you carry inside.

He's watching and waiting
patiently for you,
To give Him your heart
is all you must do.

Don't let your pride
stand in the way,
A life surrendered to Jesus
is truly the better Way.

March 20, 2014

Jesus is the Answer

Though tests in life
are sure to come,
Though the questions change
the answer is only One.

Through trials and adversity
and uphill climbs,
The answer remains constant
time after time.

In plenty or in want
in good times or bad,
In times of elation
or times quite sad;

In sickness or in health
in joy or despair,
The common thread is Jesus
He's always there.

In times of pain
in times of sorrow,
When it seems there is
no hope for tomorrow;

To the questions, problems,
stresses and strife,
Jesus is the answer
to the worries of life.

He'll lighten your burden
and carry your load,
He makes straight the path
of life's long, winding road.

Jesus is the answer
He holds the key,
In all life's conflicts
He's all we'll ever need.

The solution to the chaos
and temptations Satan hurls,
Jesus is the answer
for a dark and hurting world.

Put your trust in Jesus
He wants to make you new,
To lead and guide you
in all you say and do.

Jesus is the answer -
Won't you call on Him today?
Jesus is the answer -
He's the Life, the Truth and the Way.

June 9, 2014

You Do Not See

I see your tweets and twitters
your each and every blog,
Pictures of your kids, your cat
and especially your dog.

I see your Candy Crush
and every mystery you solve,
And each and every item
that you post upon your wall.

I wonder how it is then
that you do not see,
The words that pour out so freely
from His heart to you, through me.

I write and share them diligently
each and every one,
In hopes that some way, somehow
another soul to Him is won.

For that which we do on earth
surely will not last,
But a life lived for Jesus
will redeem us from our past.

The free gift of salvation
for all who will partake,
Secures for us a future home
within Heaven's Gates.

So as you go through life
Living from day to day,
Remember that life with Jesus
is surely the better Way.

March 22, 2014

Set Apart

Though gifted with sight
they cannot see the proof,
Though their ears hear the words
they don't comprehend the Truth.

The evidence is clear
to all who believe,
For we have seen the Light
And chosen to receive.

The free gift of salvation
and His unfailing love,
Jesus gave to all so selflessly
when He left His throne above.

Laying down His life
as He hung upon the tree,
To give the gift of eternal life
to all who will believe.

As Christians, we've a mandate
to go and share God's word,
'Til every creature, everywhere
finally has heard;

Of the depths of His love
His mercy and grace,
'Til the message of God's Word
has touched the whole human race.

We don't take His command lightly
to fulfill it is not a choice,
For now that He is gone
His followers must be His voice.

So please listen if you will
with an open heart and mind,
To the message of God's love
that transcends space and time.

For we who are His children
share the desires of His heart,
His will that none should perish
but forever be set apart.

May 26, 2014

The Hardest to Reach

I write these words
so each one will know,
When this life is over
where he will go.

Each one must decide
what he will do,
The choice is simple
there are only two:

Eternity in Heaven
for those who receive,
Or eternity in Hell
forever to grieve.

We're put on this earth
to serve our fellow man,
Each uniquely created
by God's own hand.

We're given an assignment
as part of His plan,
Each given the opportunity
to speak up and take a stand.

Those whom we love
we want so badly to teach,
But those precious souls
are the hardest to reach.

They know all about us
they know us so well,
They've seen us succeed
and they've seen us fail.

Surely they can see
the new man we've become,
Since we gave our lives to Jesus
God's one and only Son;

Who came to earth
from Heaven above,
Freely giving His life
to prove His love.

A life lived for Jesus
assures us a new home,
Where one day we will see Him
seated upon His throne.

Right this moment
He's calling to you,
To surrender to Jesus
is what you must do.

And when this life is over
to Heaven you'll go,
We know this is true
God's Word tells us so.

March 27, 2014

Turn to Jesus

In times of great sorrow
or deep despair,
There's One you can turn to
who'll always be there.

With everyday problems
you can no longer cope,
There's One you can turn to
who'll give you new hope.

When your heart is empty
there's no love to share,
There's One you can turn to
who'll always care.

You're weary from struggling
all by yourself -
Turn to Jesus,
He wants to help.

Life throws you a curve
you don't understand -
Reach out to Jesus,
He'll take your hand.

Turn to Jesus
He'll show you the way,
He'll walk there beside you
throughout each day.

Through the darkness
and into the light,
Jesus will lead you
in all that is right.

Turn from your ways
and give Him your heart,
The Savior will help you
to make a new start.

Jesus will lead you
with His power and might,
To the land of milk and honey
and eternal light.

November 26, 1993

Christ and Christ Alone

My heart cries out in anguish
yearning to be heard,
To bring to a dark and hurting world
the message of God's Word.

To open ears that will not hear
and eyes that will not see,
To soften hardened, prideful hearts
and bring them victory.

God sent His one and only Son
to die on Calvary,
And pay the ransom for our sin
to set the captives free.

Knock and the door will open -
seek and you will find,
For in Christ and Christ alone
can we surely find peace of mind.

How can I make them listen?
How can I make them see?
Through Jesus Christ alone
can we forever be truly free;

From the burdens and the struggles
the shackles and the strife,
For Christ and Christ alone
holds the key to eternal life.

January 7, 2014

The Depth of God's Love

For God so loved the world that he gave his one and only Son, that who-ever believes in him shall not perish but have eternal life. John 3:16

But he was pierced for our transgressions, he was crushed for our iniqui-ties; the punishment that brought us peace was on him, and by his wounds we are healed. Isaiah 53:5

Salvation is found in no one else, for there is no other name under heaven given to mankind by which we must be saved. Acts 4:12

And being found in appearance as a man, he [Jesus] humbled himself by becoming obedient to death–even death on a cross! Philippians 2:8-11

Do you think I cannot call on my Father, and he will at once put at my dis-posal more than twelve legions of angels? Matthew 26:53

Christ redeemed us from the curse of the law by becoming a curse for us, for it is written: "Cursed is everyone who is hung on a pole [cross]." Galatians 3:13

The Depth of God's Love

The depth of God's love
we can't comprehend,
But His love alone
can forgive all our sin.

Freely giving His Son
to die on a cross,
Providing the Way
that none should be lost.

Sin incurs a debt
that each life must pay,
Through Jesus there's redemption
He's the Life, the Truth, and the Way.

The depth of His suffering
cuts like a knife,
Jesus gave His all
to give us new life.

Mocked, scourged
and falsely accused,
His make-believe trial
was only a ruse;

To silence a man
who spoke only the Truth,
And lived a sinless life
from the days of His youth.

Nailed hand and foot
on the cross of a tree,
Jesus freely gave His life
to redeem you and me.

May 30, 2014

Selfless Act of Love

That selfless act of love
pierces to the core,
When we truly understand
the pain and suffering Jesus bore.

Knowing the price He paid
could I continue in my sin,
Or reject His gift of salvation
my eternal life to win?

How could I not be changed
when I met Him at Calvary,
Where He pardoned all my sins
and gave me victory;

Over sickness, sin and death
over hell and the grave?
My future He secured
for I am no longer enslaved.

Jesus' selfless act of love
prepared for you and me,
A pathway to the Father,
a home with Him eternally.

Fellowship with the Father
is granted to everyone,
Who truly seeks to know Him
through Jesus Christ, His son.

He knows everything about you
and yet you've nothing to fear,
He's waiting for you now
to reach out and draw near.

A simple, heartfelt prayer
is really all it takes.
Won't you surrender to Jesus now
before it is too late?

February 28, 2014

Jesus Could Love Even Me

Living for the moment
thinking only of myself,
Seeking worldly pleasures
comfort and wealth;

With no thought of tomorrow
or what it might bring,
Always taking from others
never giving anything;

A heart filled with anger
pain and deceit,
Playing with fire
consumed by its heat;

On the road to destruction
I did not see,
How through it all
Jesus could still love me.

He loved me
when no one else would.
He loved me
when no one else could.

Wandering in darkness
I did not see,
How Jesus
could still love me.

I gave Him my heart
and sought His face,
I felt His love
His warm embrace.

He sent His angels
to watch over me,
They hovered around
though I could not see.

Shielding me from danger
and guarding my path,
He showed me love and mercy
when I deserved His wrath.

Led by the Light
now I can see,
How Jesus
could love even me.

January 15, 1994

God Still Speaks

God still speaks
as He did in days of old,
Bringing joy to our heart
and peace to our soul.

In the quiet moments
you can hear His voice,
To choose to listen
is each man's choice.

God still speaks
to a yielded heart,
His blessings and comfort
He freely imparts.

He speaks words of assurance
to those who doubt,
His words are gentle.
He does not shout.

God still speaks
to those who believe,
Speaking words of solace
to those who grieve.

To the poor in spirit
God is near,
Speaking words of comfort
to erase all fear.

God still speaks
to those who mourn,
To heal a heart
that's broken and torn.

When you choose to believe
you've made the right choice,
In the quiet moments
you can still hear God's voice.

March 17, 2014

Only His Love Remains

He sees each tear as it slides
silently down your cheek,
He knows what's in your heart
when there are no words left to speak.

He knows all the feelings
you carry deep inside,
The pain and loneliness
you try so hard to hide.

He knows your dreams
your hopes and fears,
All your thoughts and deeds
throughout all your years.

He was there from the beginning
He'll be there in the end,
He's waiting and longing
to be your best friend.

This friend is Jesus
of whom I speak,
A friend to the lowly
the humble and meek.

He's waiting to greet you
with outstretched hands,
This man named Jesus
Son of God and Son of Man.

For He alone can save you
and forgive all your sins,
He wants to dwell within you
if you'll only let Him in.

He'll live in your heart
and show you the way,
To live holy and abundantly
each and every day.

He's prepared a place
for all who believe,
A home in Heaven
you'll never have to leave.

Won't you listen for
and answer His call?
Living wholly for Him
is the greatest accomplishment of all.

For worldly pleasures
and wealth won't sustain,
When all is said and done
only His love remains.

January 31, 2014

All He Had to Give

At any moment in time
from the Manger to the Cross,
God could have changed His mind
and given up on redeeming the lost.

He didn't have to send His Son
to die on Calvary,
but gave the very best He had
to set sinful captives free.

Oh how it must have broken God's heart
to see His Son nailed to that tree,
but in giving up His own life
Jesus gave new life to me.

The skies grew dark, the earth did rumble
The veil was torn in two,
Jesus freely gave His life
as redemption for me and you.

Though legions of Heavenly Hosts
were at His beck and call,
Jesus gave us all He had to give
to be our all in all.

January 19, 2014

The Same Jesus

The same Jesus
who turned water into wine,
The same Jesus healed the sick
and cured the blind.

The same Jesus
who raised man from the dead,
The same Jesus
wore a crown of thorns upon His head.

The same Jesus
who gave His life to atone for our sins,
The same Jesus
rose from the grave to live again.

The same Jesus
who lived two thousand years ago,
The same Jesus
will save you and make you whole.

His personal invitation
is open to all,
If you listen with your heart
you will hear Him call.

For every life
He does cherish,
It is His will
that none should perish.

Jesus is the same
yesterday, today and forever,
To spend eternity with Him -
there is no greater treasure!

This same Jesus
wants to know you,
Give your life to Him
and watch what He'll do!

February 20, 2014

The Bridge

Jesus is the bridge
from a life of sin and death,
To a future home in Heaven
and a life of eternal rest.

Jesus is the bridge
from darkness into Light,
To a life of contentment
free from struggle and strife.

Jesus is the bridge
from weeping and sorrow,
Jesus is The Light
our bright hope for tomorrow.

Jesus is the bridge
from confusion and moral decay,
He will surely show you
that there is a better Way.

Jesus is the bridge
from sickness to health,
From weakness to strength
and poverty to wealth.

Jesus is the bridge
to a future secure,
A life of abundance
and a love that endures.

Jesus is the bridge
between God and man.
Will you cross that bridge today?
Are you ready to take a stand?

February 27, 2014

The Jesus I Know

The Jesus I know has eyes of compassion that see beyond my circumstance right into my very soul.

The Jesus I know has ears that listen intently and hear even my unspoken cries and petitions.

The Jesus I know has lips that speak to me softly, gentle words of comfort and encouragement.

The Jesus I know has broad shoulders that share my burdens and lighten my load.

The Jesus I know has strong but gentle arms that embrace me with His love when my heart is wounded and broken.

The Jesus I know has nail-scarred hands that reach out to beckon me home.

The Jesus I know has a heart overflowing with pure love, which He pours out in equal measure on all who come to Him.

The Jesus I know has powerful legs that carry me when I'm too tired and weak to continue on my own.

The Jesus I know has wounded feet that go before me leading and guiding me as I travel the road of life.

The Jesus I know has forgiven all my sins and washed me clean by the power of His shed blood.

The Jesus I know has prepared a place for me in Heaven where I will live with Him eternally.

Do you know The Jesus I Know?

January 28, 2014

The Voice of God

The voice of God
still speaks today,
So many times
in so many ways.

We may not hear Him
in a bush afire,
For that may not be
His desire.

God reveals Himself
in subtle ways,
For no man can live
and see His face.

We can hear God's voice
in a newborn's cry,
We can hear His voice
in a loved one's goodbye.

He works in ways
we may not understand,
We must trust His heart
when we cannot see His hand.

But we can surely see
the works of His hands,
Everywhere we look
across this great land.

He spoke into being
the seven continents and seas,
And when He finished
with them He was pleased.

In the plants and animals
of vast array,
God's handiwork
is ever on display.

Ablaze with color
with texture and scent,
Where ever you look
God's work is evident.

The voice of God
still speaks today,
So many times
in so many ways.

Listen with your heart
rather than your ears,
For it is with your heart
His voice you'll clearly hear.

In times of sorrow
we feel God's love,
Pouring down like rain
from the heavens above.

In times of despair
we can hear Him say,
"I'm here today and
I'm here to stay -

Not only when you're
afraid or alone,
I want to make your heart
my forever home."

March 19, 2014

Victory

Beaten and bruised
then nailed to The Cross,
When He said "It is finished!"
it seemed all was lost.

He became sin
who knew no sin,
The victory over death
and the grave to win.

Three days later
the stone was rolled away,
And the Savior walked the earth
for another forty days.

He'd risen from the dead
it could not be denied,
They saw His nail-scarred hands
and the wound in His side.

Jesus is the provision
by which man can be saved,
There is no other one
only Jesus is The Way.

No man comes to the Father
but through the Son,
Through His death and resurrection
the Victory He's won.

Victory over sin,
death, hell, and the grave,
For whosoever will
Jesus came to save.

March 13, 2014

How Majestic is Your Name

O Lord, Our Lord
How majestic
Is Your name
In all the earth!

Alpha and Omega
The Beginning and the End,
Yahweh, Addonai,
Savior, Healer, Friend.

The Great Shepherd
The Son of Man
The Holy One
The Great I Am.

El-Shaddai, Elohim,
Messiah, Abba Father,
King of Kings, Lord of Lords,
Fountain of Living Water.

Fortress, Foundation,
Most Upright;
Comforter, Cornerstone,
Lord Jesus Christ.

Man of Sorrows
Spirit of Truth,
Ruler, Advocate,
Son of God, Firstfruits.

Teacher, Witness,
Redeemer, Guide;
Jehovah-Jireh,
Majesty on High.

Master, Deliverer,
Creator, Dayspring,
Prophet, Priest,
Servant, King.

O Lord, Our Lord
How majestic
Is Your name
In all the earth.

April 4, 2014

All Eyes are Watching You

Do not conform to the pattern of this world, but be transformed by the renewing of your mind. Then you will be able to test and approve what God's will is – his good, pleasing and perfect will. Romans 12:2

Dear friends, I urge you, as foreigners and exiles, to abstain from sinful desires, which wage war against your soul. Live such good lives among the pagans that, though they accuse you of doing wrong, they may see your good deeds and glorify God on the day he visits us. For it is God's will that by doing good you should silence the ignorant talk of foolish people. 1Peter 2:11-12, v.15

Then we will no longer be infants, tossed back and forth by the waves, and blown here and there by every wind of teaching and by the cunning and craftiness of people in their deceitful scheming. Ephesians 4:14

I press on toward the goal to win the prize for which God has called me heavenward in Christ Jesus. Philippians 3:14

All Eyes Are Watching You

As Christians we're not perfect
we just try to do what's right,
We must keep pressing on
and never give up the fight.

As Christians we must stand up
to defend God and His Word,
Bringing the message of The Gospel
to a lost and hurting world.

As Christians we're not called
to judge who's wrong or right,
But to lead them with His love
to the path of eternal life.

As Christians we are judged
on every thought and deed,
Every unsaved eye is watching
to see how we proceed;

Through times of adversity
or heartbreak and despair,
They're watching what we do
to see if we truly care.

Do we actually extend ourselves
and go out of our way,
Or do we simply commiserate and
half-heartedly offer to pray?

As Christians we have a responsibility
to bring honor to Christ's name,
To live our lives as He did
should be our highest aim.

The world is watching and waiting
to see what we will do,
Make sure that you are worthy
for all eyes are watching you.

March 10, 2014

A Faith That Cannot Be Moved

The spirit of confusion
divides God's people,
Those lacking discernment
soon become feeble.

False teachers and doctrines
are everywhere,
Promoting Satan's lies
entangled in his snare.

We must listen to God's voice
and not that of man,
We must follow His truths
drawing a line in the sand.

Even the elect
can be deceived,
Falling back into sin
causing God to grieve.

We must learn for ourselves
the veracity of God's Word,
Rather than relying on others
and the things we have heard.

We must study to show
ourselves approved,
Being grounded in a faith
that cannot be moved.

Fighting the good fight
pressing on toward the prize,
Seeking God's wisdom -
not falling for the lies.

June 3, 2014

The Ultimate Goal

A yearning and longing
within each human heart,
Was placed there by God
from the very start.

An insatiable hunger
needing to be filled,
An unquenchable thirst
to follow His will.

God placed this need
within each heart and soul,
To fellowship with Him
and receive blessings untold.

We fill this need
with worldly pleasures,
Satisfying our flesh
and acquiring earthly treasures.

But peace is not found
in wealth and fame,
or in worldly possessions
of high acclaim.

These things, my friend
are a temporary cure,
You need fellowship with God
for only His love endures.

This yearning and hunger
can never be filled,
'Til you give your life to Jesus
and do as He wills.

God sent His Son
to provide for you a way,
To have fellowship with Him
each and every day.

No one comes to The Father
but through His Son,
There is no other way
Only Jesus is The One.

He'll satisfy your hunger
and fill your empty soul,
For eternal life with Jesus
is the ultimate goal.

February 21, 2014

Sunday Morning Christians

Sunday after Sunday
we lift our voice to You,
Going through the motions
doing what we've been taught to do.

But, do we really listen
to the words we say?
Have they touched our hearts and lives?
Have we changed from yesterday?

Do we reach out to the lost
to help them find their way?
Do we show the love of Jesus
in all we do and say?

Are we there for our brother
to lend a helping hand?
Do we take the time to listen
or try to understand?

Have we given everything
and laid it at Your feet?
Would you find in us a pure heart
if today Lord, we should meet?

Are we led by the Spirit,
in peace, joy and love;
Offering prayers of thanksgiving
to the Lord God above?

Teach us Lord to listen
and answer to Your call.
Dwell within our hearts and minds
that we may never fall.

Help us Lord to be more
than Sunday Morning Christians,
To live our lives for You Lord
in truth and Godly wisdom!

July 7, 1997

The Harvest

There's no time to rest
there's work to be done.
The harvest is ripe
there are souls to be won.

They're searching and wandering
with no sense of direction,
They know not of Jesus
His life, death, and resurrection.

Like sheep to the slaughter
they've been led astray,
They need to know Jesus
He'll show them the Way.

All Christians are called
to do our part,
To lead the lost to Christ
and a change of heart;

To turn from their sin
in these last days,
To live their lives for Jesus
the Life, the Truth and the Way.

We must each do our part
for our time here is short,
Judgment Day is coming
where God will hold court.

The righteous to be judged
and awarded a crown,
The sinner too
will now finally bow down;

And surrender with pleadings
but it will be too late,
In rejecting God's Son
they securely sealed their fate.

March 25, 2014

Open My Eyes

Open my eyes
that I might see,
The truth of Your Word
that can surely set me free.

Open my ears
to hear Your voice,
To lead and guide me
in making the right choice.

Open my heart
that I might receive,
The fullness of Your love
and firmly believe.

Open my mouth
and help me to speak,
And witness with boldness
to those who are weak.

Use me Lord
to do Your will,
While I am waiting
humble and still.

I want to see with Your eyes
to love with Your heart,
I'm ready Lord
to make a new start;

To see what You see
to feel what You feel,
An unconditional love
with fervency and zeal;

To know Your mind
and know Your heart,
With a burning love
that will never depart.

And one day soon
I'll see You face to face,
And reside with You in Heaven
surrounded by Your love and grace.

February 1, 2014

What Difference Can I Make?

Keep me in Your will Lord
and keep me in Your way,
In everything I do
and everything I say.

May something that I say or do
at least in some small way,
Help lead a lost and weary soul
to turn to You today.

To a hardened and wounded heart
what difference can I make?
A kind word, a caring smile
could be all it takes.

A moment of compassion
can cause a change of heart,
That leads one to repentance
and to make a brand new start.

Keep me in Your will Lord
and keep me in Your way,
In everything I do
and everything I say.

For the unsaved are watching
to see if I fall or sway,
Or hold fast to my beliefs
and live them day by day.

March 20, 2014

Live This Day

Live in the moment
forget about the past,
Today is fleeting
it will not last.

The past you can't change
the future you can't control,
Indeed, there is no guarantee
that you will even grow old.

From moment to moment
or day to day,
Your life can change
in unexpected ways.

Live fully each day
it could be your last,
Life's clock is ticking
ever more fast.

Say a kind word
do a good deed,
Find a way
to meet someone's need.

For we're all here
to help one another,
The chance may come only once
there may never be another!

So live this day wisely
and make it count,
For one day in the future
to God you'll account;

For what you did
or did not do,
With each precious day
He gave to you.

December 22, 2013

Look Outside Yourself

When your heart is hurting
no solace to be found,
Take a look outside yourself
and blessings will abound.

Look around and see the need
for others are hurting too,
If you seek, you will find
there's something you can do.

To ease the pain or meet the need
to lighten a heavy load,
And help a fellow weary traveler
along life's winding road.

So when you're feeling down and out
the burdens too much to bear,
Take a look outside yourself
and show someone you care.

Soon you'll find you're not alone
your problems are not so great,
You'll find joy in helping others
as upon the Lord you wait.

December 18, 2013

Time with God

Time spent with God
is never wasted,
In Him you'll find a peace
you've never before tasted.

Take time to visit
with Him each day,
He'll enhance your life
in each and every way.

Dive into His word
and search His heart,
In Him you'll find a love
that will never depart.

The Alpha and Omega
the Beginning and the End,
Won't you call on Him today?
He's waiting to be your friend.

January 7, 2014

Live Holy and Wholly for Him

When conflicts and strife
descend upon your life,
And darkness
envelops your soul;

When stern, harsh words
pierce your wounded heart,
Achieving
their intended goal;

When questions abound
and doubts arise,
Search His word
and see with your own eyes;

The truths and promises
only He can fulfill,
Stay strong in His word
and follow His will.

He'll teach you and guide you
and show you the Way,
To live holy and wholly
for Him each day.

See with His eyes
and listen with His heart,
Stay strong in the Lord
that you may never part.

January 11, 2014

In Name Only

There are Christians in name only
who know all the right words to say,
And there are Christians who truly walk the walk
and live the life each day.

The Christian in name only
set out to change his mind,
But failed to surrender his heart
and leave his old self behind.

The Christian in name only
failed to spend time in God's Word,
He does not really know God
whose voice he has not heard.

The Christian in name only
does not bear much fruit,
For he knows in part only
but not the entire truth.

The Christian in name only
really doesn't have a clue,
That he must turn away from sin
and begin his life anew.

The Christian in name only
is really no Christian at all,
And only serves to contribute
to keeping unbelievers from the call.

The Christian in name only
simply sullies Jesus' name,
He misses out on God's blessings
and has only himself to blame.

There's more to being a Christian
than to simply claim His name,
You must change your way of life
you cannot remain the same.

To call yourself a Christian
you must turn from your life of sin,
And totally surrender all you have
and all that you are to Him.

March 20, 2014

Faith and Works

Doing good deeds
and being kind to one another,
Reaching out to a stranger
and uplifting our brother;

Feeding the hungry
and clothing the poor,
These things we must do
of that, I am sure.

Though these acts are noble
their worth tried and true,
But to live in Heaven
there's more you must do.

Surrender your heart
and confess your past sins,
Give your life to Jesus
and live wholly for Him.

The Bible says faith
without works is dead,
But works alone
will not get you ahead.

Faith comes by hearing
God's story of old,
Through the pages of the Bible
His message unfolds.

Faith and works
go hand in hand,
To fulfill God's purpose
and salvation's plan.

April 2, 2014

Each New Day

Each new day
holds a brand new start,
To refresh our minds
and renew our hearts;

To relinquish the past
and press on toward the prize,
To learn from our mistakes
and become discerning and wise.

Each new day
provides another chance,
To change people's lives
and improve their circumstance;

Opportunities to reach out
to help our fellow man,
And show them the need
to repent and be born again.

Repenting and turning
and beginning life anew,
Accepting Jesus as Savior
is what each must do;

To have peace and joy
and days free from strife,
The promise of abundance
and eternal life.

Don't forfeit the chance
to begin life anew,
Today's a new day
and Jesus is calling you.

Use each day wisely
for time is short,
Spend your time judiciously
on things of good report.

Store up your treasures
in Heaven above,
Spend your time here on earth
sharing God's love.

April 10, 2014

Stand Firm

Jesus is the same
yesterday, today and tomorrow,
We must take up our cross daily
our Savior to follow.

We must stand firm
we must not be swayed,
By the times and trends
and mores of the day.

His words are truth
and do not change,
They must not be distorted
or convincingly rearranged;

To appease our selfish
sinful flesh,
We must not give in
and fail the test.

We must stand firm
and fight the good fight,
And in all our conduct
be moral and upright.

The harvest is plenty
but the workers are few,
There are souls to be won
there's much work to do.

We must stand firm
we cannot be swayed,
We must lead the lost
to the Life, the Truth and the Way!

June 5, 2014

Mixed Messages

Hot one day
and cold the next,
Our mixed messages
are sure to vex;

The unseen eyes
that secretly watch,
Our everyday actions
which we frequently botch.

And unseen ears
which oft' overhear,
Our harshly spoken words
that ring out loud and clear.

We say one thing
but do another,
Serving only to perplex
and confuse each other.

An unsteady Christian
tossed to and fro,
Has failed to mature
to blossom and grow.

Our mixed messages
can do so much harm,
He'd prefer us hot or cold
rather than lukewarm.

We must be diligent,
we must be steadfast;
Cultivating a relationship
with Christ, which will last.

So share God's message
loud and clear,
A message the world
is longing to hear.

A message of hope,
peace, joy and love;
Of a Savior sent
from Heaven above.

If we live our lives
with these attributes,
A lost, hurting world
will surely follow suit.

August 3, 2014

The Power of the Tongue

Death and life
are in the power of the tongue,
Its effect immediate
its reach far-flung.

There's power in the tongue
for evil or good,
And often its intent
is misunderstood.

Its words can bring joy
and make us feel glad,
Its words can cause pain
making us angry or sad.

There's power in the tongue
to soothe or heal,
There's power in the tongue
to wound or kill.

Our words can build up
or our words can tear down,
Creating a smile
or causing a frown.

Blessing and cursing
flow from the same lips,
Use your words
to fortify and equip.

Pepper your speech
with love and hope,
Providing encouragement
to those who can't cope.

Words once spoken
cannot be taken back,
The effect they produce
can alter a life's track.

Make sure your words
are gentle and kind,
The scars they may cause
can last a lifetime.

Keep your thoughts
on God above,
And from your tongue
will flow words of love.

August 13, 2014

The Least of These

Whatever you did
for one of the least of these
you did for Me.

I was alone
and you befriended me.
I was troubled
and you brought me peace.
I was downhearted
and you brought me laughter.
I was afraid
and you comforted me.
I was weak
and you gave me strength.

I was different
yet you did not disapprove.
I was confused
yet you did not criticize.
I was uneducated
yet you did not ridicule.
I was unattractive
yet you did not taunt.
I was slow
yet you did not mock.

I was hungry
and you fed me.
I was thirsty
and you quenched my thirst.
I was barefoot
and you gave me shoes.
I was sick
and you prayed for me.
I was imprisoned
and you visited me.

I was lost
and you shared the Good News!

Whatever you did not do
for one of the least of these
you did not do for Me.

August 17, 2014

Be Not Deceived

The great dragon was hurled down – that ancient serpent called the devil, or Satan, who leads the whole world astray. He was hurled to the earth, and his angels with him. Revelation 12:9

The god of this age [Satan] has blinded the minds of the unbelievers, so that they cannot see the light of the gospel that displays the glory of Christ, who is the image of God. 2 Corinthians 4:4

The thief comes only to steal and kill and destroy: I have come that they may have life, and have it to the full. John 10:10

Be alert and of sober mind. Your enemy the devil prowls around like a roaring lion looking for someone to devour. 1 Peter 5:8

You belong to your father, the devil, and you want to carry out your father's desires. He was a murder from the beginning, not holding to the truth, for there is no truth in him. When he lies, he speaks his native language, for he is a liar and the father of lies. John 8:44

For our struggle is not against flesh and blood, but against the rulers, against the authorities, against the powers of this dark world and against the spiritual forces of evil in the heavenly realms. Ephesians 6:12

For false messiahs and false prophets will appear and perform great signs and wonders to deceive, if possible, even the elect. Matthew 24:24

The Battle in Our Mind

When fears assail
and doubts arise,
Be not dismayed
be not surprised!

For as sure as the night
follows the day,
The enemy's at work
to lead us astray;

Filling our thoughts
with foolish lies,
He feeds off our insecurities
our greed and our pride.

Satan is the antagonist
of the battle in our mind,
He beckons to us all
leaving no one behind.

He can bring us down
or falsely build us up,
Of toying with our emotions
he never gets enough.

Satan roams the earth
to do as he will,
Seeking only to destroy
to steal and to kill.

For worldly pleasures
are only temporary,
But he'd have us believe
quite the contrary.

We must not succumb
to his temptations and wiles,
They'll only rob our joy
and steal our smile.

If he can fill us with pride
and make us believe,
That of a Savior
we have no need;

Then he's completed his mission
and accomplished his goal,
Satan's achieved his objective
and won our soul.

April 22, 2014

Out of the Darkness

Come out of the darkness
and into the Light,
Give no credence to the enemy
but give your life to Christ.

Satan's lies are perpetuated
with one thing in mind,
To separate man from God
to wander in darkness for all time.

Satan's ways are crafty
and to some may seem right,
But his goal has one intention
to keep you from the Light.

If he can deceive you
and fill your heart with pride,
If he can confuse you into thinking
the way is not narrow, but wide;

He's done his job
and succeeded quite well,
In convincing you to join him
for eternity in Hell.

Don't listen to his lies
or fall into his snares,
Give your life to Jesus
the One who really cares.

Man's ways are not God's ways
and God's ways are not man's,
But God's is the better Way
through salvation's plan.

For each man must pay
the debt for his sins,
At The Cross, Jesus paid them
that we all might live again.

He laid down His life
your ransom to pay,
Give your life to Jesus
Today is the day!

Come out of the darkness
and into The Light,
To the land of milk and honey
and eternal life.

February 24, 2014

It All Started With A Bang

Theories come and theories go
with no reason or no rhyme,
But God's Word is never-changing
and has stood the test of time.

How can you believe
that it all started with a bang?
When God finished His creation
I'm sure all of Heaven sang;

Rejoicing in the majesty
of the works of His hand,
The sky, the seas, the rivers
the mountains and dry land.

From the giant redwoods and sequoias
to the tiniest grain of sand,
Each unique in its own way
subject to The Master's hand.

In the dark expanse of the heavens
each star He hung in place,
And with tender loving care
He created the human race.

Created in His own image
yet no two exactly alike,
He saw that man was alone
and created for him a wife.

The complexity and variety
of every living thing,
Could simply not have evolved
from one gigantic bang.

From the warm summer sun
to the fresh scent of the air,
In the animals, trees and plants
I see God everywhere.

The beautiful colors of sunset
or a newborn baby's cries,
Everything God created
is a feast for our ears and eyes.

The infinite, finite details
of every living cell,
With its intricacies and complexities
their own unique story to tell.

How can you believe
that it all started with a bang?
Take a look around
you'll see God's touch in everything.

For to deny God's existence
His deity, power and might,
Must be the saddest condition
of all human life.

To believe yourself wiser
than the Great Creator,
Of all life's travesties
there could be none that's greater.

In denying God's existence
you also tie His hands,
You stop the flow of blessings
and miss out on His divine plan.

For God has a trajectory
for your life to follow,
A life of joy and abundance
no more in mediocrity to wallow.

How can you believe
that it all started with a bang?
God created this world for you
to bless you with everything.

March 7, 2014

Don't Blame God

Circumstances change
nothing stays the same,
When things don't go our way
God often gets the blame.

He works behind the scenes
preparing the way,
Directing our path
through each night and day.

God's plans we can't foresee
some can be misunderstood,
But He works all things together
for our own good.

His ways are not our ways
some we can't understand,
So we must trust His heart
and His divine plan.

We must walk by faith
and not by sight,
Trusting in God
to make all things right.

We must place our trust in Him
and firmly believe,
In losing our faith
we cause the Spirit to grieve.

So, don't blame God
when things don't go your way,
He's working His plan.
You'll understand one day!

June 6, 2014

Be Not Deceived

Even the elect
can be led astray,
It happens so often
in these last days.

We've forgotten the truths
we've frequently heard,
So we justify our deeds
our thoughts and our words.

False teachers and doctrines
are everywhere,
Drawing us deeper and deeper
into the enemy's snare.

If he can convince us
what's wrong is right,
In deceiving a believer
Satan's won the fight.

Study to show
thyself approved,
Establishing a faith
that cannot be moved.

Though trials and adversity
may assault and assail,
A saint grounded in The Word
will always prevail.

Be not deceived
by what may seem right,
Take up your cross daily
and follow the Light.

God's words are true
they have not changed,
Though many have come
and thoughtfully rearranged;

His words and their meaning
to appease sinful flesh.
Do not fall for Satan's lies
and fail the test.

You've come too far
to turn back now,
Stay immersed in God's Word
He'll show you how;

To discern His truths
and not be led astray,
Assured of receiving your crown
on Judgment Day.

March 27, 2014

The Evidence

How can you not believe
that Jesus is God's Son?
How can you not believe
He is the Chosen One?

The signs are all there
woven throughout God's Book,
The evidence is clear
if you'll only take a look.

Born of a virgin
in the town of Bethlehem,
He gave His life on a tree
to pay the ransom for our sin.

He caused the blind to see
and made the lame to walk,
The deaf He made to hear
the mute He caused to talk.

Betrayed by a friend
and rejected by man,
A few pieces of silver
placed Him in the soldiers' hands.

Jesus is The One
who was nailed to The Cross,
Providing a path of redemption
for all the world's lost.

Sin incurs a debt
for which a price must be paid,
There is no other path
only Jesus has the power to save.

The evidence is plain
but you must choose to believe,
Do not listen to the enemy.
Do not be deceived.

Satan's mission is simple
to destroy, steal and kill,
He'll use any means necessary
to keep you from God's will.

He wants you to question
he wants you to doubt,
He wants your soul lost
he wants you to miss out;

On all the many blessings
God has planned for your life,
The free gift of salvation
and the promise of eternal life.

The evidence is there
in the pages of God's Book,
Won't you pause for a moment
and simply take a look?

God's will is that none should perish -
not one be left behind.
Won't you open now your heart
your spirit and your mind;

To the power of God's love
and the truth of God's Word?
It contains the most important message
the world has ever heard!

March 13, 2014

Whenever I Call

Sacrifice thank offerings to God, fulfill your vows to the Most High, and call on me in the day of trouble; I will deliver you and you will honor me. Psalm 50:14-15

So do not fear, for I am with you; do not be dismayed, for I am your God. I will strengthen you and help you; I will uphold you with my righteous right hand. Isaiah 41:10

You, LORD, are forgiving and good, abounding in love to all who call to you. Psalm 86:5

Indeed, the very hairs of your head are all numbered. Don't be afraid; you are worth more than many sparrows. Luke 12:7

The LORD himself goes before you and will be with you; he will never leave you nor forsake you. Do not be afraid; do not be discouraged. Deuteronomy 31:8

I called to the Lord, who is worthy of praise, and have been saved from my enemies. 2 Samuel 22:4

Stop for a Moment

In the hustle and bustle
of your everyday life,
Stop for a moment
and simply enjoy being alive.

Linger and listen
as the morning birds sing,
Stop and reflect
as distant church bells ring.

Savor the cool
crisp morning air,
And the smell of the wind
as it tousles your hair.

Take time out
away from the crowds,
To simply notice the blue sky
with its soft, billowy clouds.

God's glory and presence
surely abound,
In every sight
and every little sound.

From the snow-capped mountains
to the verdant hills and plains,
In adorning His creation
God did not refrain.

From the glory and promise
of a new sunrise,
Everything God created
is pleasing to the eyes.

Stop and reflect
upon all God has done,
He loves us so much
that He gave Jesus, His Son.

For whosoever
believes upon Him,
Is given eternal life
and the forgiveness of sins.

So stop for a moment
and make your future secure,
Give your life to Jesus
for it's His love that endures.

March 6, 2014

The Cure

The words of the Bible
are true and sure,
To all of life's problems
its pages hold the cure.

The hurting receive comfort.
The lonely find a friend.
The troubled attain peace
that never shall end.

Sinners are forgiven.
Wandering souls are led.
The fearful receive courage.
Hungry spirits are fed.

Imprisoned souls gain freedom.
The weary find rest.
The foolish acquire wisdom.
The mediocre become God's best.

Those in darkness see the Light.
The redeemed receive favor.
The weak are strengthened.
The lost find a Savior.

The sick are healed.
The tempted overcome.
Through Christ the Savior
the victory is won.

The words of the Bible
are true and sure,
To all of life's problems
its pages hold the cure!

April 7, 2014

God Knows

God hears your silent prayers
offered deep in the night,
And sees your wounded heart
yearning to take flight.

He sees the single tear
slide slowly down your face,
And feels your lonely soul
longing to be embraced.

God knows your insecurities
your weaknesses and doubts,
He knows what makes you smile
and sing and dance and shout.

He's numbered every heartbeat
and hair upon your head,
He knows your every thought
and every word you've said.

God knows where you are going
and everywhere you've been,
Every good thing you have done
as well as every sin.

He knows your whole life's story
all the challenges and strife,
Your victories and accomplishments
along this journey of life.

God knows everything about you
from the beginning 'til the end,
But all He'll ever ask of you
is to know you and call you friend!

February 28, 2014

Your Heart for His Home

A heart now hardened
by loneliness and tears,
Rejected and abandoned
year after year;

An empty spirit
devoid of hope,
A battered soul
that can no longer cope;

Disillusion and despair
heartache and grief,
Longing and searching
for a moment of relief;

A glimmer of hope
a ray of sunshine,
Yearning for a love
that will last through all time;

A love unconditional
with no strings attached,
Only looking forward
forgetting about the past.

Such love can be found
in Jesus alone,
If you'll open your heart
and give Him a home.

He'll quietly knock
at the door of your heart,
When you let Him in
He'll give you a new start.

Out with the old
and in with the new,
Turning from sin
is all you must do.

He'll bring peace and joy
you've never before known,
If you allow Jesus to use
your heart for His home.

March 13, 2014

Whenever I Call

Though time after time
I stumble and fall,
Jesus is waiting
whenever I call.

Though I may wander
or sometimes stray,
When I call out to Him
He's never far away.

Reaching out to embrace me
with His loving arms,
To shield me from danger -
to rescue me from harm.

He's given His angels
charge over me,
When I call out His name
the enemy must flee.

He's there in my sorrow
my pain and grief,
Offering His love
His comfort and relief.

I cannot touch Him
or see Him here,
But I know He lives
His presence is clear.

In my heart I believe
and my spirit affirms,
Our bond is secure
our commitment long-term.

Jesus gave me His life
so I gave Him my heart,
Now His love assures me
that we'll never part.

April 8, 2014

He Knows Me Better

Through the plastic smile
and brightly painted eyes,
Jesus saw the real me
I tried so hard to hide.

He knew all my thoughts
all my hopes and fears,
He saw all my weakness
and all the shed tears.

He felt the pain
and sorrow I felt,
He knows me better
than I know myself.

He entered the darkness
and bathed it with light,
Forgave all my sin
and gave me new life.

He taught me to worship
and praise His name,
And from that day on
I was never the same.

That which was hidden
is no longer concealed,
Great mysteries unfold
as the Spirit reveals.

Things I tried on my own
only to fail,
Now He is with me
and all is well.

He shares all my burdens
and shows me the way,
He walks there beside me
throughout each day.

Each morning a new song
plays in my heart,
For I know that Jesus and I
will never part.

October 31, 1993

His Name is Jesus

His eyes see the pain
and tears of sorrow,
The aching and longing
for a brighter tomorrow.

His ears hear the cries
of despair and regret,
The pleas for help
and for needs to be met.

His heart knows our troubles
and all of our cares,
He's right there with us
all our burdens to bear.

His hands reach down from Heaven
through the annals of time,
Bringing peace and comfort
to weary souls and minds.

His strong but gentle arms
embrace the brokenhearted,
With a bond of love
that cannot be parted.

His feet carry us softly
wherever we go,
He walks there beside us
as we travel down life's road.

Do you know this man
of whom I speak?
He's a friend to the lowly
the mild and the meek.

He's waiting to meet you
to show you the Way,
To live life to the fullest
each and every day.

His name is Jesus.
Won't you take His hand?
He alone can lead you
to the Promised Land.

And when your life is over
no longer this earth to roam,
Jesus, and the God of Heaven
will be waiting to welcome you Home.

January 16, 2014

Your Dearest Friend

We navigate life alone
and put God on a shelf,
'Til one day we finally realize
how desperately we need His help.

We think that we are wise
and can do it on our own,
'Til we grow so weary from struggling
that our heart has turned to stone.

When our pride and independence fail
and our spirit becomes weak,
It's in these times of struggle
that His face we finally seek.

And surely we will find Him
waiting with open arms,
For He delights in helping His children
and keeping them safe from harm.

God wants to know us intimately
and share our every care,
To guide us through life's challenges
safe from the enemy's snare.

He wants to be a part
of every decision that we make,
Seek His counsel daily
from the moment you awake.

Open up your heart
and invite Jesus in.
No need to struggle alone,
He'll be your dearest friend.

February 28, 2014

Forgive Our Unbelief

When our life falls apart
all torn and tattered,
It's in these moments
that our faith can be shattered.

We like the loose ends
tied neatly in a bow,
When we don't understand
it's a tough row to hoe.

We all question our faith
from time to time,
Searching for answers
when there's no reason or rhyme.

We question and ponder
what we don't understand,
Even doubting our faith
when we can't see God's hand.

Our pain or circumstance
can drive us apart,
Leaving us confused
with a heavy heart.

His ways are not our ways
some we can't understand,
But we must trust His heart
and His divine plan.

God's will for us
is His perfect peace,
And He alone
can heal all our grief.

We know all things work together
for our own good,
When we meet God in Heaven
His plan will be understood.

So in our time
of pain or grief,
Forgive us Lord
our unbelief.

April 19, 2014

Run to Jesus

When you're ready to quit
the going's too rough,
You can't take any more
it's just too tough.

Your heart won't survive
another heartbreak,
You've given all you have
there's nothing left to take.

You've tried everything
but to no avail,
If you try again
you'll continue to fail.

Run to Jesus
He'll show you the Way,
Guiding your path
with each new day.

Run to Jesus
in your pain and sorrow,
He'll give you the strength
to face a new tomorrow.

Run to Jesus
for He understands,
And holds you securely
in the palm of His hands.

March 16, 2014

On Our Knees

Birth, graduation
Marriage, empty nest,
Reunion, retirement
and eventually death;

Life's milestones
come and go,
In a constant
ebb and flow.

Yet, the defining moments
are not found in these,
Life's defining moments
are found on our knees.

Time alone with God
is so often the key,
To finding contentment
and security.

When many facets of life
seem out of control,
Our time alone with God
will fortify our soul.

On our knees
when we pour out our heart,
God's always willing
to make a fresh start.

On our knees
we find peace and strength,
And find God will go
to any length;

To bring us joy
and satisfy our soul,
Sharing His blessings
and riches untold.

On our knees
we're closest to Him,
Where Jesus can cleanse us
and forgive all our sin.

Time on our knees
is a precious time,
In time on our knees
we see God's light shine.

09/02/14

I'll Weep No More

...weeping may stay for the night, but rejoicing comes in the morning.
Psalm 30:5

The LORD is close to the brokenhearted and saves those who are crushed in spirit. Psalm 34:18

"I have told you these things, so that in me you may have peace. In this world you will have trouble. But take heart! I have overcome the world."
John 16:33

He will wipe every tear from their eyes. There will be no more death or mourning or crying or pain, for the old order of things has passed away.
Revelation 21:4

Surely he took up our pain and bore our suffering... Isaiah 53:4

Then we which are alive and remain shall be caught up together with them in the clouds, to meet the Lord in the air; and so shall we ever be with the Lord. 1 Thessalonians 4:17 (KJV)

A Heart Breaks

A heart breaks quietly
and no one hears,
A heart breaks in darkness
and no one sees the tears.

A heart breaks in silence
it has no voice,
A heart breaks in despair
it has no choice.

A heart breaks quickly
as life turns on a dime,
A heart breaks slowly
with the passage of time.

A broken heart
needs time to heal,
To forget the pain
and allow itself to feel.

A broken heart
is slow to mend,
Afraid to trust
and love again.

A broken heart
is fragile and meek,
Afraid to be open
again to speak.

When finally one day
the two parts become one,
Love again burns brightly
as the noonday sun.

February 13, 2014

Memories

A familiar face at rest
in its final repose,
The heart must accept
what the head already knows.

The heart now remembers
and frequently calls to mind,
So many forgotten memories
over the long expanse of time.

Longing, searching eyes that locked
across a crowded room,
To share a lifetime of memories
that ended all too soon.

Two hearts that beat as one
over a span of many years,
One left alone to carry on
through emptiness and tears.

A broken heart keeps beating
until its final day,
Searching again for happiness
all along life's way.

For some there may be another
for others there's only one,
But memories will sustain us
'til our time on earth is done;

And we meet again in Heaven
where there will be no more tears,
Two hearts again united
through all the millennial years.

March 12, 2014

I'll Weep No More

I still can't believe you're gone
for I clearly see your face,
In the pictures of my mind
that time cannot erase.

The twinkle in your eyes
the curve of your lip,
Your grin from ear to ear
at some funny little quip.

Your hands I never realized
looked so much like mine,
Now seem to meld together
with the steady passage of time.

All the words still unspoken
all the things still undone,
How could I have known that that day
would be your final one?

The sun rose in the east
and settled in the west,
But sometime in between
God called you home to rest.

You took with you a part of me
that cannot be replaced,
Until I see you once again
standing at the Pearly Gates.

The day is coming soon
when I'll weep no more,
And I'll meet you there in Heaven
to share all God has in store.

February 5, 2014

Until Then

I long to see you once again
and hear the sound of your voice,
To go back to the day you left
and write the ending of my choice.

I look in the mirror and see your face
your eyes, your nose, your smile,
Oh how I long to feel your touch
to sit and hold you for a while.

To laugh, to talk, to giggle
or to simply reminisce,
There are so many, many things
about you two I miss.

I know today you're happy
and free from all the pain,
But from the moment that you left us
nothing's been the same.

Your cozy, comfy chair
is a vacant lonely place,
There's a huge hole in my heart
that time cannot erase.

Thank God for His promise
to see you once again,
In my new home in Heaven
at this journey's end.

I know you'll be there waiting
with Jesus at The Gate,
Though we do not know the time
and we do not know the date.

So Mom and Dad, until then
you'll live on in my heart,
Anxiously awaiting the day
we'll no longer be apart.

February 3, 2014

Just Another Day

The secret pain
and unshed tears,
Lingering just below the surface
each day throughout the year;

At Christmastime are magnified
and brought into the light,
As I lie in bed awake
yet another sleepless night.

A heart can feel so heavy
and yet empty at the same time,
Searching for an answer
but finding no reason or no rhyme.

Though Christmas
is a time of joy,
Celebrating the birth
of a baby boy;

For some it is a time
of pain or sorrow,
Clinging to the hope
of a brighter tomorrow.

People passing on the street
too busy to stop and see,
Beyond the cheerful laugh or smile
to the brokenness inside of me.

So as you go along
your merry little way,
Remember that for some
Christmas is just another day.

December 16, 2013

My Christmas Wish

If I were granted
one Christmas wish,
I'd go back in time
to see all those I miss;

To see their smile
and touch their face,
To give them a hearty
warm embrace.

Remembering the merry
Christmases past,
Reliving the joy
I thought would always last.

The tinsel and lights
that once shone so bright,
Now that they're gone
nothing seems quite right.

To go back in time
and experience once more,
The excitement and joy
of walking through their front door;

To sit there beside them
and hold their hands,
As we talk and remember
and share life's plans.

So many memories
live now only in my heart,
And life's just not the same
since we've been apart.

I know you had to go
I can even understand why,
Yet every time I think of you
a tear still fills my eye.

But I will not be sad
I will not be blue,
For I know that one day
again I'll see you.

So until then
you'll live on in my heart,
'Til we meet there in Heaven
never again to part.

December 22, 2013
Merry Christmas ~ Mama and Daddy

Eternity

Just as people are destined to die once, and after that to face judgment, so Christ was sacrificed once to take away the sins of many; and he will appear a second time, not to bear sin, but bring salvation to those who are waiting for him. Hebrews 9:27-28

Nothing impure will ever enter it [Heaven], nor will anyone who does what is shameful or deceitful, but only those whose names are written in the Lamb's book of life. Revelation 21:27

My Father's house has many rooms; if that were not so, would I have told you that I am going there to prepare a place for you? John 14:2

Very truly I tell you, whoever hears my word and believes him who sent me has eternal life and will not be judged but has crossed over from death to life. John 5:24

Now this is eternal life: that they know you, the only true God, and Jesus Christ, whom you have sent. John 17:3

Eternity

When your life is drawing to a close
and you look back and reminisce,
Recalling the things you should have done
and the opportunities you missed.

I pray there was a time in your past
when you asked Jesus into your heart,
A day you can look back on
when you made a brand new start.

With God, it's never too late
up 'til the moment of death,
He gives us all a chance to come
'til we draw our final breath.

But death is an unpredictable thing -
it often comes without warning.
If this should be your final night -
where will you awaken in the morning?

Will you find yourself in Paradise
to live eternally with Him?
Or have you never made this choice -
the consequences of which are grim?

Make your decision while you can,
the chance may not come again!
Jesus is waiting with open arms
to save you and forgive all your sins.

This is the appointed hour.
Now is the time to choose.
You have eternal life gain
or everything to lose!

February 5, 2014

Final Destination

My name's in The Book
I have my reservation,
Some day I'm going home
to my final destination.

He secured my place
as I knelt at The Cross,
Surrendering to Jesus
a life that was lost.

He forgave all my sins
and washed me anew,
Asking Him to be my Savior
was all I had to do.

His promises for me
are also for you,
Won't you come to Him now
without further ado?

He's waiting to meet you
with nail-scarred hands,
He'll prepare for you a home
in the Promised Land.

Humbly receive Him
into your heart,
Today is the day
to make a new start.

Your name too
can be written in The Book,
Come to Jesus now
without a backward look.

You've nothing to lose
and everything to gain,
An eternal home in Heaven
forever with Him to reign.

You too, my friend
have a final destination,
Take the time today
to make your reservation.

February 2, 2014

The Answer

Troubled and weary
with nowhere to turn,
Inside, anger
and hatred burned.

A heart full of grief
I'd lost all hope,
Feeling I could
no longer cope.

Walking blindly through life
but going nowhere,
Running from the past
about the future I did not care.

The burdens were many
and pleasures too few,
At the end of my rope
what else could I do?

Thinking it would be so easy
to just end it all,
When faintly I heard
a gentle voice call;

He said, "The answer is here
in this book in your hand,
Inside you will find
salvation's plan;

If you'll repent of your sins
and turn from your ways,
You can be one
in the Kingdom today."

So I knelt at His feet
He took my hand,
I cried out for mercy
He said, "I understand."

Right there and then
I gave Jesus my heart,
I said, "I'm ready, Lord
to make a new start."

He cleansed my heart
he forgave all my sins,
And gave me new life
that I might live again.

He said, "I know where you've been
the things you have done,
But today my child,
you and I became one."

August 20, 1993

This Could Be The Day

With the stresses of life
you can no longer cope,
The situation looks dim
and you've lost all hope.

Lost and weary
mixed emotions churn,
Afraid and confused -
Which way should you turn?

You've tried everything
to no avail,
In going it alone
you continued to fail.

Put your trust in Jesus
He'll show you The Way,
To live a life of abundance
day after day.

He'll guard your path
and lighten your load,
He'll fill your life with joy
and riches untold.

Knock and the door will open.
Seek and you will find.
Make your decision now
before you run out of time.

This is the hour
and this is the place,
For this could be the day
when you finish the race.

Is your name written
in the Lamb's Book of Life?
Have you received the gift of salvation
and the promise of eternal life?

March 10, 2014

Finally Home

I've arrived safely home
at my final destination,
My passage booked at the altar
as I received the gift of salvation.

That day my name was written
in the Lamb's Book of Life,
And today I left my earthly body
to begin eternal life.

My time on earth passed quickly
in the twinkling of an eye,
I lived a long, full life
but you know how time flies.

As I closed my eyes on earth
angels carried me away,
When I opened them again
I was standing at Heaven's Gate.

Long gone friends and loved ones
met me at the Gate,
Rejoicing at the decision I made
that securely sealed my fate.

The foundation of the walls
is layered in precious stone,
And I walk on streets of gold
in my new heavenly home.

In Heaven there's no darkness
no need of sun to light the day,
The pure glory of the Lord
brilliantly lights the way.

Every color of the rainbow
radiates from God's throne,
Angelic songs of praises ring
throughout my new home.

The crystal-clear river
of the water of life,
Flows from the throne of God
past the tree of life.

I saw His nail-scarred hands
and the wounds in His feet,
There are no tears in Heaven
therefore I did not weep.

As I knelt at His feet
my soul did rejoice,
To see Him face to face
and hear His gentle voice.

So do not weep for me
for I am finally home,
Seated at the feet of Jesus
who reigns upon His throne.

March 22, 2014

Choose This Day

But if serving the LORD seems undesirable to you, then choose for your-selves this day whom you will serve... Joshua 24:15

No one can serve two masters. Either you will hate the one and love the other, or you will be devoted to the one and despise the other. You cannot serve both God and money. Matthew 6:24

At that time people will see the Son of Man coming in clouds with great power and glory. And he will send his angels and gather his elect from the four winds, from the ends of the earth to the ends of the heavens. Mark 13:26-27

And the devil, who deceived them, was thrown into the lake of burning sulfur, where the beast and the false prophet had been thrown. They will be tormented day and night for ever and ever. Revelation 20:10

He will punish those who do not know God and do not obey the gospel of our Lord Jesus. They will be punished with everlasting destruction and

shut out from the presence of the Lord and from the glory of his might... 2
Thessalonians 1:8-9

*Jesus answered, "Very truly I tell you, no one can enter the kingdom of
God unless they are born or water and the Spirit." John 3:5*

*The Lord is not slow in keeping his promise, as some understand slowness.
Instead he is patient with you, not wanting anyone to perish, but everyone
to come to repentance.* 2 Peter 3:9

Whom Will You Follow?

Disappointed, disillusioned
and fed up with life,
No longer content
to just merely survive;

Longing and searching
for meaning and purpose,
Weary of the rat race
and three-ringed circus;

Repeatedly chasing
empty pipe dreams,
Buying into deceptions
and crazy schemes;

Running in circles
and getting nowhere,
You've lost all hope
and you just don't care.

But do not give up
and do not despair!
There's Someone who's greater
than all your cares!

With open arms
He's waiting for you,
He wants to cleanse you
and make you brand new.

To turn and repent
is all He requires,
He'll give you His peace
and your heart's desires.

He'll give your life meaning
and purpose anew,
To surrender to Jesus
is all you must do.

Time is short
with no promise of tomorrow.
Decide today!
Whom will you follow?

June 5, 2014

The Choice Only You Can Make

We can be a friend of God
or a friend of the world,
So the Bible tells us
as His Word unfurls.

We cannot serve
both God and man,
And expect a place of honor
at His right hand.

With every decision
there's a right and wrong,
With every choice
we must be strong;

To choose what is right
and be not led astray,
For wide is the gate
but narrow is the Way.

So choose wisely
whom you will serve,
On this road of life
with its bumps and curves.

The end of your road
you could reach today.
Have you joined with Him
in the better Way?

When you close your eyes
for the very last time,
Will you awaken in Heaven
to a new life sublime?

The choice is one
only you can make.
It's up to you
which road you will take.

Please make your choice
right here and now.
The decision is easy
I'll show you how.

Trust in Him
with all your heart.
Today is the day
to make a new start.

If you'll repent of your sins
and turn from your ways,
your place in the Kingdom
is secured today.

His life for you
He freely gave,
So that you too could conquer
death, hell and the grave.

February 1, 2014

Choose This Day

Choose this day
whom you will serve,
Choose the God of Heaven
for He's the God you deserve.

For you cannot serve
both God and man,
You must make a choice.
You must take a stand.

Don't cheat yourself
and don't miss out,
For one day God's children
will ascend with a shout.

Some day Jesus will come
to carry us home,
No more in darkness
on this earth to roam.

What more could He do?
What more could He give?
His very life He sacrificed
that you may forever live.

With all the successes
and accomplishments you've known,
If you've never met Jesus
you've forfeited your heavenly home.

Surrender to Jesus
and live in the Light,
With the power and assurance
of eternal life.

March 5, 2014

Heaven or Hell?

My heart cries in despair
my soul in anguish weeps,
For all the lost souls
the enemy herds like sheep.

Our husbands and wives
our sons and daughters,
Follow him blindly
like lambs to the slaughter.

They say there is no God
but they've been deceived,
The fact of their perishing
makes my heart grieve.

Their eyes do not see
their ears do not hear,
They know not the God
who I feel so near.

They think I am weak
they think I am wrong,
But I know God is real
His love is so strong.

I pray God reveals
Himself to them too,
I've said all I can say
and done all I can do.

The choice is there
for each one to make,
I pray they choose wisely
for eternity's at stake.

Each man is free
to choose Heaven or Hell,
The choice each one makes
only time will tell.

April 10, 2014

Dear Reader

I pray that God, through these words, has touched your heart, your mind, and your soul.

If you are already a believer, I pray that you have been encouraged, renewed and strengthened.

If you are presently a non-believer, I pray that the Holy Spirit is speaking to your heart. I urge you to yield to Him and surrender your will, your heart, and your life to Jesus now. It is the most important, life-changing decision you will ever make.

If you are not yet ready to surrender your life to Christ, I pray that you are prompted to seek a deeper understanding of Him. I would suggest you start by reading the Gospel of John in the New Testament of the Bible.

If, at any time, you feel God calling you to repentance and to begin a new life in Christ, all you need to do is pray this simple prayer.

Dear Lord Jesus~

I know I am a sinner. I believe that you are the Son of God and that you died for my sins. Right now, I turn from my sins and ask you to forgive me and cleanse me from all unrighteousness. Come into my heart to rule and reign. I receive you as my personal Lord and Savior. Thank you, Lord, for saving me. ~ Amen

Now, go and tell someone of your decision so that they may rejoice with you. Begin to read the Bible and spend time with God each and every day. Join a Bible-believing, Bible-teaching church in your local community and be baptized.

Begin to watch Christian television. I highly recommend David Jeremiah (Turning Point), Joyce Meyer (Enjoying Everyday Life), John Hagee (John Hagee Today), Kerry Shook (Kerry Shook Ministries), Jimmy Evans (Marriage Today) and Greg Laurie (Harvest Ministries). I believe all of these programs air on TBN network – many are shown daily.

I also urge you to begin listening to Christian music on the radio. God ministers to us mightily through music. You will quickly find yourself humming or singing along as your spirit soars and your heart rejoices.

May God Bless and Keep You!

Yours in Christ ~

Kathy

CPSIA information can be obtained
at www.ICGtesting.com
Printed in the USA
LVOW07s0233171217
560064LV00003B/420/P